# Dinosaurs

## Kathleen Weidner Zoehfeld

**SCHOLASTIC INC.**
New York  Toronto  London  Auckland
Sydney  Mexico City  New Delhi  Hong Kong

## For Whitley

ISBN 978-0-545-45177-2

Copyright © 2011 by National Geographic Society.
All rights reserved. Published by Scholastic Inc., 557 Broadway, New York, NY 10012,
by arrangement with National Geographic Society. SCHOLASTIC and associated
logos are trademarks and/or registered trademarks of Scholastic Inc.

12 11 10 9 8 7 6 5 4 3 2          13 14 15 16 17/0

Printed in the U.S.A.          40

First Scholastic printing, February 2012

All illustrations by Franco Tempesta unless otherwise noted below:
5, 32 (bottom, left): © Will Can Overbeek/ NationalGeographicStock.com; 6-9, 23, 32 (bottom, right)
© Louie Psihoyos/ Corbis; 11 (top, left): © Brooks Walker/ NationalGeographicStock.com; 11 (top, right
© Xu Xing; 18: © James Leynse/ Corbis; 20: © Francois Gohier/ Photo Researchers, Inc.; 26-27: © Kar
Havlicek/ NationalGeographicStock.com; 28: © Joel Sartore/ NationalGeographicStock.com; 29: ©
National Geographic/ NationalGeographicStock.com; 31: © Paul Bricknell/Dorling Kindersley/ Gett
Images; 32 (top, right): © Lynn Johnson/ NationalGeographicStock.com

# Table of Contents

# Big Scary Bones!

Have you ever seen dinosaur bones in a museum (mew-ZEE-um)? Some of them are huge! If those bones came to life, it would be pretty scary.

But not to worry. All the big, scary dinosaurs died off long, long ago.

The bones weren't always at the museum. Where did they come from?

**Word Bites**

MUSEUM: A building where you can see dinosaur bones and other rare and important things

# Digging Up Dinosaurs

The dinosaur bones were buried safely in rock for a long time.

The bones are fossils (FOS-uls). Paleontologists (pay-lee-on-TOL-o-jists) found them. They dug them out of the ground.

## Word Bites

**FOSSIL:** Part of a living thing that has been saved in stone

**PALEONTOLOGIST:** A scientist who finds and studies fossils

They brought the fossil bones to the museum and cleaned them. Then they put them all together.

Bones were on the inside of a dinosaur. But what did dinosaurs look like on the outside?

# Dinosaur Skin

Sometimes dinosaur skin left prints in mud. The mud hardened and saved the prints.

These fossils tell us that some dinosaurs were scaly, like lizards.

**Triceratops**
(tri-SER-ah-tops)

skin fossil

feather fossil

And some dinosaurs had feathers, like birds.

**Buitreraptor**
(BWEE-tree-RAP-tore)

# Dinosaur Superstars

**Tyrannosaurus rex**
(ty-RAN-oh-SORE-us REX)
was one of the biggest meat-eaters
that ever walked the Earth.

**Diplodocus**
(dih-PLOD-uh-kus) was one of
the longest dinosaurs ever found.

**Pachycephalosaurus**
(pack-ee-SEF-ah-loh-SORE-us)
walked on two legs and
had a thick, domed head.

## Triceratops

(tri-SER-a-tops) had a huge head with three large horns and a wide neck frill.

## Ankylosaurus

(AN-kye-loh-SORE-us) was an armored dinosaur. It had a solid bone club at the end of its tail.

## Stegosaurus

(STEG-oh-SORE-us) had rows of tall plates running down its back. Its tail had four deadly spikes.

# Smallest Dinosaurs

When you go to the museum, be sure to look for the smallest dinosaurs.

Some are small enough to hold in your hands. Many small dinosaurs had feathers.

*Microraptor*

You

# *Microraptor*

(MIKE-ro-rap-tore)

# Biggest Dinosaurs

The biggest dinosaurs were the long-necked sauropods (SORE–uh–PODS). You can't miss them! Sauropods like *Argentinosaurus* are the biggest land animals that ever lived.

**Argentinosaurus**

**You**

## Argentinosaurus
(ahr-gen-TEEN-oh-SORE-us)

# Walking on Tiptoes

knee

Big or small, scaly or feathery—all dinosaurs walked on their toes.

ankle

toes

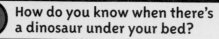

**Q** How do you know when there's a dinosaur under your bed?

**A** Your nose hits the ceiling!

And all dinosaurs had curvy, S-shaped necks.

neck

*Edmontosaurus*
(ed-MON-toh-SORE-us)

# What Did Dinosaurs Eat?

A dinosaur's teeth tell us what it ate. *Brachiosaurus* and *Diplodocus* were plant-eaters. They had dozens of chisel-like teeth. Their teeth were good for snipping tough branches.

fossil of *Diplodocus*

# *Brachiosaurus*
(BRACK-ee-oh-SORE-us)

# Deinonychus
(die-NON-e-kus)

Other dinosaurs were meat-eaters. They ate other animals.

*Deinonychus* had teeth as sharp as steak knives. They were perfect for slicing meat.

tooth of meat-eater
*Tyrannosaurus rex*

# Dinosaur Moms and Babies

All dinosaurs, even the
scariest meat-eaters, laid eggs
and had babies.

Some of them, such as
*Oviraptor*, guarded their nests
and kept their eggs warm.
When the babies hatched, the
parents looked after them
until they were big enough to
live on their own.

# Oviraptor

(OH-vih-RAP-tore)

# Is THAT a Dinosaur?

Lots of people think anything big and dead is a dinosaur. But that's not right.

Is this a dinosaur?

**woolly mammoth**
(WOOL-ee MAM-uth)

No! The woolly mammoth was huge. But this animal did not lay eggs like a dinosaur. And it had fur. No dinosaurs had fur.

The woolly mammoth lived after the big dinosaurs went extinct (ik-STINKED).

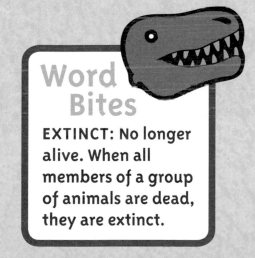

Word Bites

EXTINCT: No longer alive. When all members of a group of animals are dead, they are extinct.

# Is this a dinosaur?

**Chicken**
living dinosaur

It walks on its toes. It has a curvy neck. It has feathers like *Anchiornis*. And it lays eggs.

Yes! A chicken is a dinosaur. All birds are living dinosaurs.

**Anchiornis**
(ank-ee-OR-niss)
extinct dinosaur

# Your Pet Dinosaur

Many people would love to keep dinosaurs as pets.

You might think a *Tyrannosaurus rex* would be fun to play fetch with. But you wouldn't want to be near it at dinnertime. And besides, it's extinct!

If you want a dinosaur of your own, look for one that's small. A small dinosaur makes a very good pet!

**EXTINCT:** No longer alive. When all members of a group of animals are dead, they are extinct.

**FOSSIL:** Part of a living thing that has been saved in stone

**MUSEUM:** A building where you can see dinosaurs and other rare and important things

**PALEONTOLOGIST:** A scientist who finds and studies fossils